FRONTIER MOTHER

FRONTIER MOTHER

By

O. GLENN STAHL

Illustrations by Kay Russ

THE CHRISTOPHER PUBLISHING HOUSE
NORTH QUINCY, MASSACHUSETTS

COPYRIGHT © 1979
BY O. GLENN STAHL
Library of Congress Catalog Card Number 79-53718
ISBN: 0—8158—0386—9

PRINTED IN
THE UNITED STATES OF AMERICA

To
MARIE JANE

PREFACE

Current attention given the status and rights of women often obscures the enormous influence that women have exerted in the past. When reminded, we recognize the significant roles played by such figures in the American colonial and revolutionary period as Abigail Adams, Betsy Ross, Martha Washington, and others who are well-known to recorded history. Seldom, however, do we learn much about less-celebrated individuals whose impact on the American family and mores, and on our national integrity, may have been just as momentous. This story, in short, is about such a woman.

The principal events in the story are factual. The characters were real people—ancestors of the wife of the author. The narrative recounts the harrowing experiences of the pioneering Reynolds family during its effort, in 1779, to migrate by riverboat from western Maryland to the region known as Kentucky.

The only recorded information on these events was that published in a Hagerstown, Maryland newspaper (*The Torch Light*) in 1835—a journal that ceased to exist some time before 1861. Printed in two lengthy articles in successive weekly issues, the story had been based on the recollections of one of the surviving Reynolds children (Elizabeth). The people involved and the main occurrences have also been verified through other sources.

This account of the trials and resourcefulness of Margaret Reynolds (Mrs. John Reynolds), Elizabeth's mother and the heroine of the story, was told to the original newswriter in 1835 when Elizabeth was sixty-four years old. We obtained possession of these two issues of *The Torch Light* because my wife (Marie Jane) is a direct descendant of Mrs. Reynolds. The two copies had been faithfully kept in the family and had finally come to Marie Jane. To our knowledge, no other source for the account detailed in this vignette of American history exists. These two old copies of *The Torch Light* are apparently the only ones available today.

With the encouragement of our daughter (Elaine Stahl Leo) I have undertaken, with some supplementary research, to flesh out the full story in some cohesive fashion. All the important features are based precisely on the original news stories. However, since the news version lacked some needed details, possibly because of the half-century interval between the events and their recording, I have fictionalized a few passages in order to fill in some awkward gaps and tie loose threads together. I have tried to do this in a manner that is consistent with the conditions, personalities, geography, and overall spirit of the time when these events were taking place. I hope that my efforts have provided a suitable bonding ingredient and given the story "an even flow" in those areas where the reader might have become confused and lost the story's logical progression from one episode to another.

The narrative has been passed on via the maternal side of each generation of Marie Jane's family, from 1835 to the present. It is testimony to the indomitable fortitude and intelligence of the pioneer American woman in the eighteenth century.

O. Glenn Stahl
Arlington, Virginia

CONTENTS

Preface	7
1. The Lure of the West	19
2. Starting Downstream	31
3. Disaster	39
4. Murderous Trek	49
5. Gauntlet	59
6. The Food Crisis	69
7. Painful Separation	75
8. Joyful Reunion	89
9. Escape	105
10. And So to Home	121
Epilogue	127

ILLUSTRATIONS

"We had better follow the streams"	23
"... where the river is wider, things should be easier	33
Margaret was more concerned about John than her own safety	41
Indians desperate not to lose any of their captives	51
There was no alternative	61
Much needed sustenance	71
A less painful respite from rigors of the forced march	79
Some degree of maternal affection	84
To howl and make all the noise in her power	91
"It's my Mama!"	101
Determined Indians had not yet given up	117
"And whose little boy are you?"	125

FRONTIER MOTHER

Chapter 1

THE LURE OF THE WEST

Margaret Reynolds was greatly relieved when her husband John returned safely after having participated in some battles with the British. She had inwardly feared for his safety on many occasions; his infrequent letters were not reassuring. Because of the uncertain means of posting letters and the long intervals before they arrived, she had often thought that he had been killed—perhaps even while his latest letter was enroute to her. Months of absence had seemed a decade to her. She had already begun to formulate in her mind various schemes for providing for their seven children. Of these, the youngest was practically a stranger to John when he did come back from the war in the early part of 1778.

Margaret was a ruggedly attractive person. Sparkling blue eyes, a ruddy but fair complexion framed with radiant light-brown hair, and a beautifully proportioned strong body had made her one of the most desirable young women in Washington County,

Maryland. This was the impression one would have gathered had he lived in that location during Margaret's formative years. But as she matured, she also became known for a quick wit and an almost flawless use of common sense. It was for both of these reasons that young John Reynolds was more than content when he won her hand. She was only sixteen, but he was the envy of every other young swain in Washington County.

The early married years of Margaret and John were prosperous ones, yielding considerable material wealth—by colonial standards—as well as a bounteous progeny. John, in addition to managing a farm of hundreds of acres, also had an interest in several local enterprises—the principal one of which was a local trading center, dealing in all the kinds of goods that were needed on the frontier and that could be transported from Philadelphia, Williamsburg, or the fledgling port of Baltimore. By the time he was twenty-seven (Margaret was then twenty-five) he already had the satisfaction of having several men in his employ. The interlude of war fortunately had found him with sufficient going concerns that a reasonably adequate living had been provided for his young family during his absence. And when he returned, he had attained the rank of Captain in General George Washington's army. This was an honor and a distinction that immediately guaranteed him the respect of both his peers and elders in Washington County.

It was a solid base of achievement on which succeeding events could be built—but which, nonetheless, could not guarantee that those events would be anything near as happy as the earlier years.

As with many young wives of the revolutionary period, Margaret Reynolds was vitally interested in her husband's economic ventures. In spite of her heavy load as a mother of seven—for which she had considerable assistance from relatives—she found time for lengthy conversations with John about his affairs of property and finance. Even the welfare of the farm animals intrigued her. It was not in a meddling or nagging way that she intruded; she was genuinely attracted by the intellectual and physical challenges, and John came to respect her judgment and counsel in the many decisions they had to share. It was only military affairs in which she had no interest whatsoever, and which she resented as a spoiling interruption in their happy domestic life.

Naturally, as talk about opportunities in the West blossomed after the War, Margaret was much involved in the frequent discussions. Trappers, traders, explorers, adventurers—all brought to their community tales of the grandeur of Kentucky, a few hundred miles to the west. True, western Maryland was not bad country for grazing; there was plenty of water, and the mountains offered some protection from the worst winds of winter as well as the scorching summers—but the prospect of gentle rolling grasslands, without too many trees to fell, was an appealing one to an enterprising young family. In brief, John, within a few months after his return from the War, felt he had secured all the satisfaction he could from Washington County. Margaret, although not quite as eager, fully understood his ambition. She could scarcely imagine, of course, the ultimate role that would befall her in pursuit of that ambition.

The decision to move westward was not a sudden announcement by John made after a particularly tender episode of love-making or some other moment of ecstasy. It was a gradual process over several months, a kind of mutual realization between husband and wife that the move was really to take place. "If ever we go west," John would say, "we had better follow the streams."

Margaret would add, "I suppose it would be safer as well as easier."

"But," John would interject, "we can't make it alone as a family."

"The Malotts and Hardens are eager to go too," observed Margaret.

Then, almost before they quite realized the monumental character of the undertaking, John was finding out about methods of reaching the Ohio River

"We had better follow the streams"

and the prospects of locating barges and boats that might navigate it. Margaret, in turn, was thinking through the lists of provisions that would have to be taken along.

If Captain Reynolds and his practical wife had not been people of some means, as the criteria of the day would have it, they could never have contemplated such a bold excursion into unknown territory. It was not primarily economic need that drove men westward in these early days; it was the wonder, the excitement, the sheer thrill of carving out an even more rewarding life in the wilderness. It was to be half a century before mass migrations by covered wagon were to mark the great plains. This earlier westward movement was more sporadic, more individual, and more dependent on having the material resources to dare to try. And there were no great plains to be traversed. Here and there some open glades, yes, but going to Kentucky meant hills, rivers, forests, and only a few open vistas. All of this multiplied the risks many times, for one never knew what lay beyond the next bend in the stream.

By late summer in 1778 the plan to move was definite. John had made arrangements with several friends to sell his property, disposing of the store separately and splitting the farm into two parts. This was necessary because so few possessed the means to buy him out in one transaction. Margaret was

THE LURE OF THE WEST 25

preoccupied with acquiring boxes and cases to store clothing, provisions, utensils, tools, and all the paraphernalia essential to living away from civilized quarters.

It became her responsibility to work out arrangements with the Hardens and the Malotts. Mrs. Harden, with two children, and Mrs. Malott, with five, were to be associated with Captain Reynolds' family, while their husbands were to travel separately. In addition, Captain Daniel Stull, Robert Dowler, Ralph Naylor, and three servants were to go along.

By now it was mid-September. The warm early-fall days were encouraging. It seemed as if the weather itself conspired to entice even those who were wavering to develop enthusiasm for the venture. Certainly there were no forebodings of the trials yet to come.

Finally, with several wagons all loaded, the valiant little party set out on an old northwesterly trail to reach the Ohio. It took over a week to cover the 150 miles or so to the tributary that was later named the Monongahela. Not far south, and upriver from the confluence with the Ohio River itself at Fort Pitt (the outpost that George Washington had established on the site that later became Pittsburgh), was a settlement known as Redstone, the community where the Reynolds party was to be quartered for the winter. Parcelled out among various families in their crude log dwellings with clapboard roofs, the group made out very well. John and Margaret were sufficiently affluent to pay for their keep and a modest rental besides.

On a diet of pork and hominy, johnny-cake and corn pone, milk and mush, occasional vegetables that had been stored from local gardens, and frequent wild meats that nearby forests offered and trusty rifles garnered, the westward-moving colony thrived through the winter. Indeed, it was a diet that was especially suited to cold weather, and, to quote a phrase that an historian coined, it "made strong men and buxom women."

Whenever there were breaks in what otherwise might have seemed a long, bleak winter, John Reynolds and his colleagues were busy scouting for flatboats and related equipment that they could use for the main part of their voyage in the spring. To supplement what she had already accumulated from back home, Margaret scoured the community for every possible item she could think of that would help sustain the group while it was waterborne. She even thought of getting three extra commodes, so that there would be adequate space for the human waste that would accrue if they were boat-bound for several days at a time. The river itself was, of course, to be the wash basin, sewage disposal, and drinking reservoir for everyone.

At first Margaret wanted to use several small barges, so that their worldly goods and children could be spread around, "without all her eggs in one basket," as she put it. But John persuaded her that two craft, requiring fewer hands to propel, were enough, with the one designed to hold the animals—to be tended by the hired hands accompanying them—and the other outfitted primarily for sleeping and eating quarters. With some difficulty John was finally able to buy one barge and commission construction of another. Also, Harden and Malott obtained two additional small boats, not much larger than rowboats. Fortunately, most of the month of February was mild enough that they could accomplish much of the outfitting of the two major craft during that period.

The other two mothers and their children plus two servant women, it was agreed, would be carried on the main barge with the Reynolds family, while some of the menfolk would superintend the smaller vessel that carried several horses, three cows, two goats, and a large crate of chickens. Harden and Malott were to man their separate boats alone.

The crisp spring days were bracing. Again, all the harbingers of the voyage about to begin were hopeful ones.

Chapter 2

STARTING DOWNSTREAM

It was the evening of March 24, a moonlit night and one somewhat warmer than those preceding. Nature's beauty and bounty seemed to grace the impending departure. The next day, Margaret's thirty-first birthday, they were to set forth. Since most of their possessions had already been carefully stored or set up for use on the main barge, the Reynolds family slept that night on rough mats that could be carried aboard the last minute with other final items. When their eldest, Joseph, had fallen asleep, Margaret and John were mindful that this might well be their last night of privacy for many days ahead. The pain of separation had already impressed itself on both of them during the war interlude. Their love and vigor could not tolerate any lengthy periods of abstinence in their uncertain future. Tired as they were, their last night's embrace was one of the most satisfying ones since John had returned over a year earlier. And they could not help whispering about tomorrow's excursion both before and after their surge of physical passion.

"Poling and paddling that big boat, even downstream, won't be easy, Margaret. We'll have to fight eddies and shoals and sandbars."

"Maybe the women can help once in a while," soothed Margaret.

"You'll have enough to do as it is," John rejoined.

She retorted, "Thank God it isn't upstream that we're trying!"

"We'll just have to rely mainly on the river current to move us along," observed John. "Once we get where the river is wider, things should be easier."

"Yes, I know." After a long pause Margaret added, "Oh, I hope everything goes well. Let's be very careful. I love you and the children so very much!"

"You can be sure I'll do my best. I love you and the children just as much. Don't worry, we'll have plenty of protection."

And so, by mid-morning of March 25, the party of venturesome Americans poled their barges and boats from the rough pier at Redstone and began navigation on the tributary to the Ohio. Fortunately there was no wind that day from the west or north, so "pushing with the current" was not countered by a force in the opposite direction. In the unwieldy craft, it took six days of substantial struggle before they reached the Ohio proper at Fort Pitt.

"... where the river is wider, things should be easier"

"Ahoy, there!" yelled Malott, "The worst is over!"

"Right you are," Captain Reynolds called back.

And Captain Stull observed, "All we need now is patience, my friends—not so much brawn."

Not to be outdone, Margaret Reynolds was ready with the quip, "Maybe here is where the women can do some of the paddling—with a stronger current!" The relief at this first stage of achievement and the general levity created a whole series of playful remarks, a lightheartedness sorely needed after nearly a week of uneventful but laborious dodging of many shallows and obstacles—and perhaps an unconscious, lurking realization of hardships still likely to come. It was time to give vent to the spirits, and indeed to uncork a few bottles of the same.

Seldom did these devout Christian outdoorsmen indulge in alcoholic drink, but there had been practicality enough in the entourage to bring along a modest case of whiskey, rum, and homemade wine— for use, to be sure, only sparingly and on special occasions. In fact, it was wise Mrs. Reynolds who first insisted that they should have such beverages aboard. "Who knows," she said, "we might even need it for medicine." And that was no joke, for such bottles were the only source of anything resembling either a laxative or an antiseptic. In any event, this was surely one of the joyful occasions for use of their modest stock purely for pleasure. But the sense of conservation also prevailed to the extent that only one bottle of whiskey was opened for the men, and one bottle of wine for the ladies. Considering that only three of the latter deigned to partake, one of them being Margaret, the women really got the better of the deal!

Although members of the party had gone ashore several times during the earlier part of the trip, when the men had managed to bring down and dress two small deer, a wild turkey, and four or five rabbits (there obviously having been no meat among their initial provisions), this was the first time the entire party had spent the better part of a day and one whole night on the banks. It was a welcome relief for the children especially, as they had felt quite pent-up in the restricted space of the barge. Some of the meat that had been cooked on the earlier land sojourns was still on hand, so this day and night in the highlands of western Pennsylvania was one of genuine feasting.

For two more weeks the little party of river craft pressed on. By now they had reached a point on the Ohio then known as Long Reach, about forty or fifty miles below the recently established settlement of Wheeling. Little of consequence transpired during this period, except that the problem of keeping the children contented continued to plague Captain and Mrs. Reynolds and their party. The confining space of even the main and largest boat was hardly enough to provide a satisfactory outlet for the energies and interests of a total of fourteen children, twelve of whom were age nine or younger. This problem indeed was significant enough to have led to a series of events that dramatically altered the entire journey.

Chapter 3

DISASTER

It was a bright morning in late April when, primarily to gratify the children, Captain Reynolds brought his main boat to a convenient spot on the south shore of the river. Before all the passengers had disembarked, the Captain, knowledgeable in the ways and signs of native American Indians, spotted various evidences that red men had been about the place no more than a short time before. In a subdued but firm voice he commanded, "Quick, back on board! There's danger. Quick now!"

Though not appreciating the character of the danger, even the smallest children heeded the order with reasonable dispatch, and the men began rowing for the center of the stream. Finally, they seemed to be safely on their way, nearly caught up with the other boats which had not made the stop. In a few moments John, having had a not-too-restful time the night before, fell asleep with his head on Margaret's ample lap. He was not aware that a natural inclination of the river was carrying his craft rather near the northern shore, nor certainly could he have been aware that a contingent of Indians had deliberately planted themselves at a point on that shore where they fully expected the boat to drift.

Suddenly, without any warning, when the barge came within range, a storm of rifle balls poured upon the unsuspecting crew. The very first volley felled one of John's helpers and one of the Harden children. Awakened by the fire, John grasped his rifle and leaped to his feet. He did not even have a chance to take aim; another shot killed him instantly. Margaret stood petrified by her slain husband while a further shower of balls whizzed about her head. The children, though in a somewhat more protected area, were terrified.

"Down, Mrs. Reynolds!" yelled Ralph Naylor, "They'll get you if you don't get down." Poor Margaret had been so distraught that she had not even noticed, until she got down behind some boxes, that one shot had penetrated her bonnet. Never having been under fire before, Margaret was more concerned about John—not yet accepting that he was beyond help—than she was about her own safety.

Meanwhile, Naylor had been able to hit one of the Indians on the shore who had unwittingly revealed himself from behind a tree. Thinking fast, he immediately dropped his empty rifle alongside John's body

Margaret was more concerned about John than her own safety

and picked up John's loaded gun, in the hope of making the Indians believe it had been the Captain who had killed one of their brethren. This stratagem paid off, for later the Indians were bent upon executing Naylor until he could demonstrate that the empty gun that caught their companion was that of the dead Captain.

Accompanied by savage-like shrieks and yells, the Indians kept up the fire. The boat was floating near the shore, its crew still unable to force it farther into the stream.

"What do you say we do?" cried Naylor to Margaret, perceiving that she was now the surviving owner of the craft. "Maybe we better surrender, ma'am; it could save a lot of lives. They've got us cornered."

Only gradually regaining her composure, Margaret answered, "Do what you think best."

Whereupon Naylor stood up and yelled, "We surrender!", only to be forced to crouch down again by renewed Indian firing. When it ceased again, he sprang out upon a corn crib at the side of the boat and again exclaimed, "We surrender!" This time he got a response.

Stepping from behind a tree one of the Indians, clapping his hands to his breast, yelled back, "Come, me good man, Delaware." At that point the concealed Indians emerged, about twenty-five of them, and came down to the water's edge. They swarmed alongside and aboard the boat and towed it to shore, fully exulting over their capture of nineteen prisoners and most of the Reynolds' posssessions. Only a few horses and cattle on the other Reynolds boat, and the occupants of the two smaller boats—which were farther downstream—had managed to escape. But it was learned later that a brother of Robert Dowler on the animal boat had also been killed, thus bringing the immediate toll of white persons slain to four.

Before much in the way of communication could be established, the Indians seemed bent upon getting their prisoners and booty off the river and on to a land trail as quickly as possible. Later it was ascertained that they had been mindful of the presence of a small party of military men downstream. Since most of the material spoils of their attack was in the form of portable dry goods, the Indians immediately loaded every white adult, some of the older children, and themselves, with boxes and packages and ordered a forced march that led along the meanderings of a deep ravine and terminated on a high point of level land. Here they encamped about sunset.

Meanwhile, the Indians had swiftly scalped the three who had been killed on the Reynolds' boat and left the bodies on the boat to continue floating aimlessly downstream. It was the eventual discovery of these remains by the aforesaid military group, and the recognition of Captain Reynolds by one of the colonels, that gave civilization back east the first report of the disaster that had befallen the pioneering party. Waving the scalps around on the ends of poles, the captors took fiendish delight in flaunting them before the terrified women and children as they marched.

At the first camp site the Indians pinioned each male member of their white captives, built several campfires, and managed to get the point across that if any of the men escaped, revenge would be taken out on the lives and welfare of the women and children. "Oh, God, don't leave us," implored Mrs. Harden, with the obvious support of Mrs. Reynolds and Mrs. Malott. Their entreaties were hardly necessary, for none of the three remaining men—Stull, Naylor, and Dowler—had any intention of forsaking them to seek their own safety. And they did hold fast to their commitment to the last.

Later it became clear that the Indian party was composed of representatives of three tribes—Delawares, Mirgoes, and Wyandots. Their leaders were known to white men as Peter and Leatherlip, the former a Delaware, and the latter a Wyandot. Whatever their ethnic origins, they were brothers all on this first triumphant encampment. Having discovered the means available on the boat, they spent most of the night in a drunken carousal that kept all but the youngest children from getting much sleep after that wearying first day of captivity. Their inebriated state provoked many fights among themselves, so that by morning they had to dress each others' wounds as well as achieve a sufficient state of sobriety to proceed with leadership of their prisoners' march.

Chapter 4

MURDEROUS TREK

The second day of the forced march of the captives was marked by renewed Indian gloating over their conquest. One tall young warrior, having come upon Captain Reynolds' regimental uniform and his watch, quickly donned the suit, pocketed the watch and, with the scalps attached to a war pole, proudly strode at the head of the whole party.

"Oh, see," he shouted, "me soldier." Odious as this parading and desecration of her husband's uniform were to her, grieving Margaret did not dare show any sign of distress or repugnance. If ever there was a time when she had to cry inwardly and curse under her breath, this was it. It was a singularly painful and frustrating experience. Coupled with the physical drain on her, her children, and her companions, Margaret's mind and spirit were tested almost to the breaking point.

Distress of the captives was seldom able to alter the enforced march as it pressed onward, day after day. Even for people accustomed to the rigors of outdoor life and occasional hardship, the trials endured on this murderous trek were greater than most Americans could possibly have withstood. Neglect of everyday needs for food, water, and body eliminations were constant sources of misery. In view of problems with communication, meeting such needs was usually agonizingly difficult, to say the least. Because the Indians were desperate not to lose any of their captives, which they obviously viewed primarily as valuable economic property, they were suspicious any time a child or adult sought refuge behind a tree to relieve himself. Food was scarce and haphazard, consisting of berries or wild fruit and infrequent ears of corn roasted over a fire. Indeed the latter came to be viewed as a rare treat, so undernourished was the party most of the time. About the only thing available in sufficient quantity was water, because the number and the spring flow of creeks and runs in this territory were bounteous.

Walking over rough ground and often through brush and tangled undergrowth caused many injuries to feet and legs. Even the children had to walk for the most part; in fact, none over the age of five years was ever carried except to ford streams. Mrs. Reynolds' youngest, William, was only a few months over three and had to be carried at least half the time on the back of one or another of the white adults who

Indians desperate not to lose any of their captives

took turns at the chore. One of Mrs. Malott's youngsters, age four and a half, was carried less frequently. The youngest Reynolds girl, Elizabeth, age eight, was only rarely carried piggy-back. Often there were fallen trees, deep ravines, and small rivulets to cross, as well as steep hills. At surmounting some of these obstacles the older children were more adept than the women, but miraculously all such impediments were overcome with only minor injuries. More serious wounds did occur later, as we shall see, but were more the result of deliberate mistreatment by the Indians than by nature's obstacles.

Sign language was the usual order of communication between whites and Indians. Although two of the Indians apparently knew a few English words, they tended to be nouns only, and their users had little notion of how to convey action except by making elaborate hand and arm motions. And, of course, except for a few words of the Delaware language known to Captain Stull (which he did not attempt to use for fear of being misunderstood or provoking some kind of resentment at any mistake), the white people were utterly unable to express themselves in any tongue with which the Indians were at home.

It was under these circumstances that this aggregation of captors and prisoners pushed on for nearly a week. The direction was generally north and west

MURDEROUS TREK 53

over what is now eastern Ohio. It soon became clear that the Indians were heading for Indian villages on the Muskingum River somewhere above the present site of Zanesville. Fortunately, the inhabitants of these towns were Delaware Indians who had been converted to Christianity by Moravians in the east and had moved out here to separate themselves from their less civilized kinfolk. But this very characteristic also opened them up to exploitation by unscrupulous Indians who were frequently passing through.

At the village of Gnadenhutten (probably a name borrowed from the Moravians) the party of bedraggled captives was allowed to rest for two nights and a day. All of the children had bruised and lacerated limbs from frequent falls, which their mothers had not been able to tend or about which they had not even been able to offer a consoling word. Hungry and almost prostrate with fatigue, both adults and children were relieved to find kind Christian squaws who knew a little English and who were much interested in tending to their needs. The good Moravians brought hominy and milk to the starving prisoners and otherwise did their best to make them comfortable in their encampment just outside the village itself. The hominy was especially relished, even though it had been made by the crude process of boiling shelled corn in lye and separating the grain from the hull by dousing in cold water.

The Indian squaws managed to explain to Margaret Reynolds and her woebegotten colleagues that in spite of their attempts at good works they (the Christian Indians) were in constant danger of their lives, being hounded on the one side by jealous white men and on the other by suspicious pagan Indians. They lived, as they termed it, "between two wild animals." These precarious circumstances were the result of the location of their little Christian enclaves on the route between pagan Indian villages to the west, and white Christian communities in Pennsylvania and western Virginia. Villages known as Salem and Shanbourn, as well as the one being visited, were natural stopping places for marauding parties of hostile Indians who wished to refresh themselves after raids on white farms to the east. These bandits would insist on leaving some of their spoils with the Moravian Indians as compensation for food and other comforts. Knowing the danger to which discovery of these articles might expose them, the Moravians would decline to receive them, only to have their criminal visitors charge them with attachment to the whites and threaten their lives. Hence the Moravians were intimidated into accepting whatever they were given.

At the same time, white men also visited these towns when in pursuit of the bands of Indians who had stolen their property and murdered their relatives. Although the Moravians treated the white people with the same hospitality they were accustomed to showing the Indians, they were often found in possession of goods which the whites could identify as belonging to their neighbors back home. Consequently the white men would accuse their hosts of committing or being accomplices in the death of those whites whose property they had. Giving the above explanation, the Moravians would avow their innocence, but suspicions would linger among many whites.

It was such circumstances, as a matter of fact, that led to thoughtless retaliation by the whites in the village of Shanbourn three years later, in 1782. Here a band of vengeful white men massacred all ninety-six inhabitants, with the mistaken belief that they were compensating for Indian raids. Of all people who deserved understanding it was these kindly Christian Indians, brethren of those who had befriended our party of captives in 1779. Yet they were mercilessly slaughtered without a chance to explain or to defend themselves. It was the classic example of how one episode of mindless violence feeds upon another and how otherwise reasonable people can inflict untold harm on innocent bystanders in their rage to "get even."

Understandably, perceiving the apprehension of their helpful hosts, the Reynolds party felt great pity for them and hoped that such retaliation by whites or Indians would never befall them. They had no way of knowing about or helping to forestall the disaster that took place three years later. With great reluctance, they left this oasis of humanity to continue toward whatever fate their captors had in store.

Chapter 5

GAUNTLET

"Where on earth are we being taken?" moaned Mrs. Malott as the refreshed party continued the trek northward. Both Mrs. Malott's and Mrs. Harden's husbands, on their separate boats, were presumed to be safe on their voyage down the Ohio, but it was the grieving Mrs. Reynolds who was called upon to offer words of encouragement.

"We'll just have to wait and see. Maybe some more Moravian villages lie ahead. We'll hope so. Though nothing will bring back my dear John."

At this kind of conversation some of the older children would be provoked to tears, even as they struggled along the precarious trail. Their route was parallel to the banks of the Muskingum, heading, as they were to find out later, toward the Sandusky area.

It was at this point in the march that the most senseless and brutal treatment of all was first visited upon the prisoners—the cruel practice of running the gauntlet. It seems that whenever the captors encountered war parties of other Indians, they were required to expose their captives to this barbaric onslaught. Although they were reluctant to meet up with such groups, for fear of losing some of their prisoners, they could not avoid all of them. This was one of those unavoidable occasions.

Between two lines of Indians who were armed with whips, clubs, ramrods, and tomahawk handles and standing about six feet apart, each prisoner was required to run to some given point at the opposite end of the line and accept whatever punishment came his or her way en route. There was no alternative. With little hesitation (men first, then women and children) they stoically raced as fast as they could through these straits of cruelty. Although some of the children were spared the hardest blows, several adults in the group were severely beaten, especially Margaret Reynolds, who received a blow on the head that broke her comb and drove one of the teeth into her scalp—an injury from which she suffered extremely for at least a month afterwards.

The adults tried valiantly to suppress their screams and moans in order not to feed the savage appetites of the warrior Indians who were seeking just such aural pleasure, but the cries and wails of the terrified children made up for their elders' self-control. The smallest children were carried by the men and

There was no alternative

shielded as best they could with their strong arms. By a stratagem, one of the young heroines in the group, eight-year old Elizabeth Reynolds, managed to escape harm in this particular gauntlet. When the beatings of the first in line began, she slipped aside and hid behind a tree, unobserved. As the prisoners gained sanctuary at the opposite end, Elizabeth was able to run to her mother's side without being molested.

The only relief to the tormented souls in the party was the discovery that they were to encamp at this spot for the night. At least they did not have to compound their injuries with immediate tortured marching. But they were forced to retire with almost no food, and the evening was rapidly turning cold. Bundled together with all the clothing and blankets they could muster, the pitiful huddles of humanity tried to sleep as best they could. Most of the children were between the women, and the men sought to surround the entire group with their own somewhat larger frames.

The next morning the creek beside which they had fitfully slept was frozen over. But no obstacle of this kind could stay the relentless Indians from pushing their party onward. They broke the ice and demanded that the captives wade across. Except for the two oldest boys, the children were all carried for this short distance. The men had to make more than one trip to keep their burdens water-free. That some of the party did not contract severe colds and pneumonia from this ordeal in icy water could only be attributed to Providence and a morning sun that rapidly warmed up as the April day progressed.

Ralph Naylor, being especially outraged at this latest hardship and indignity, muttered under his breath to Margaret Reynolds, "Is there no end to their devilment? We could easily have gone upstream a piece where the water is shallower. I hope that icy blast caused you no harm."

"It was awful, but my head hurts so bad from that gauntlet yesterday, I almost wish I could have dunked it in the water to freeze the pain out," countered Margaret. "And I do hope to God the children don't suffer from this weather. I never knew it to be so cold in April in Washington County. We must be farther north than I suspected."

"We must be approaching the lake region," observed Robert Dowler, having overheard the under-the-breath conversation. Actually they were still short of the Indian village where Zanesville now stands. Mrs. Harden and Mrs. Malott were so put out by the freezing experience that their teeth were chattering, effectively braking their infrequent efforts at speech.

Later in the day the party was presented with another natural obstacle. This was Will's Creek, a branch of the Muskingum, a stream far too deep to ford. With some leadership and insistence by Daniel Stull, the white men and the Indians cut down a large tree that reached across the creek, forming a makeshift footbridge, over which the entire party crossed. Many years later, when Elizabeth was a middle-aged woman, she was visiting this part of Ohio and discovered the very stump that had been left showing the marks of Indian hatchets. Her memory was further authenticated by the local folklore that accurately portrayed the site as the place where the footbridge was fashioned for a group of Indian captives.

On the next day the group finally reached the Indian village, where again they were obliged to run a warriors' gauntlet. On this occasion Captain Stull, with little William Reynolds on his shoulder, came near losing his life. How the child escaped unhurt was something of a miracle, for he was covered with blood from the poor Captain's head. Stull never actually recovered from this abuse. Though he lived to return eventually to his friends and relatives, he was ever after subject to mental lapses from time to time—resulting no doubt from a seriously fractured skull.

Little Elizabeth was not so fortunate in this gauntlet. She not only had to run but to take her full share of the flogging. Had she not been assisted by her older sister, Mary, who urged her on more rapidly,

Elizabeth would have undoubtedly suffered more.
On top of all these hardships the Reynolds family suffered still another tragedy. It is not clear exactly where along the line this occurred, but the fact of its occurrence is indisputable. At some point during the forced march one of the Indians became interested in Margaret's oldest boy, Joseph, who was now approaching his thirteenth year. Somewhere along the line he was spirited away and taken north into Canada without his mother's full awareness of the time or circumstances of his departure. She had not been paying as close attention to him and his needs as she had the others for the simple reason that he was the one child in the best position to fend for himself. It was just shortly after they had left the last Indian village that she became aware of his absence. Through some cunning, one or more of the Indians had whisked him away from the main party. No doubt he was considered of special value, because he was approaching adolescence and was a sturdy, handsome young fellow.

So much had caved in on the poor woman in a rapid sequence of calamities that Mrs. Reynolds could hardly comprehend what all had happened. She was almost numb from shock. Losing Joseph meant she had lost the one individual who was the most likely to substitute for her husband in a protective role. Being conscious of this concern was the closest she came to a selfish thought, but to deny that it briefly crossed her troubled mind would be to attribute a kind of sainthood to her nature that could hardly be expected of the most selfless of persons.

But we must return to the chronology of the tragic march.

Chapter 6

THE FOOD CRISIS

From the last gauntlet to Upper Sandusky, the party came very near starving to death. The stock of provisions was so exhausted that the adult whites were entirely without food for more than two days, and the small children were reduced to a daily allowance of one spoonful of gruel made of parched corn. Little Elizabeth fell to the ground on more than one occasion, largely due to weakness. Her mother was herself so fatigued and hungry that she could afford her no assistance. In fact, Margaret's imagination almost became uncontrollable; she feared that in Elizabeth's helpless state the merciless Indians might well dispatch the child with a tomahawk, leaving her body in the wilderness to be devoured by beasts of prey. Only the firmest resolve not to succumb to such horrid fantasies kept her from complete derangement. She pulled her thoughts together sufficiently to pray to Almighty God that no further grief would befall her or her children. It took all the bravado she could

muster to avoid any behavior or word that would
call attention to the child's plight, lest she awaken
the already suspicious Indians to suppose Elizabeth
could go no farther and thus seal her fate. Then,
looking over her shoulder, Margaret had the unspeakable pleasure of seeing Elizabeth get up again from
her last collapse, aided by her faithful, brave sister.
And there came to Margaret's mind a verse she had
learned as a child:

> "Sweet fraternal care!
> That twining bound two souls in one."

Unknown to the prisoners, the Indians had sent a
part of their company ahead to Upper Sandusky to
procure food—the timely arrival of which saved the
whole party from starvation. Each person, white
and Indian alike, was meted out one pint of parched
corn meal, mixed with cold water and sweetened
with sugar. Strengthened by this much needed sustenance, the group moved on slowly until it came
near to Sandusky.

Here some of the Indian company separated from
their companions without ceremony and took with
them one of Mrs. Malott's little daughters, Blanchy,
and Mrs. Reynolds' six-year old son, John. Mrs.
Malott immediately conceived that it would be wise
for one older child to go along and suggested that

Much needed sustenance

one of the Reynolds girls accompany them. With a flourish of pointing and other motions, she urged her view upon one of the Indians with considerable vehemence. Becoming irritated at the "white squaw's" impertinence, the old Indian signaled that he differed with her by the well-known sign of the uplifted tomahawk. On seeing this the disappointed mother could only retreat and hold her peace. Neither of the two mothers, distraught as she was, was allowed the privilege of an affectionate embrace of farewell with her respective offspring.

It seemed that no sooner was one occasion of tribulation overcome than they were almost immediately confronted with another. In comparison with losing one's child even starvation seemed tolerable. Each day brought a new twist of fate or Indian cunning that shattered those small sparks of hope that still flickered in their breasts. At this stage, then, Margaret had not only lost her loving husband for good, but also two of her boys to an uncertain fate, with the lurking prospect that still more of her progeny would be separated from her. Yet, with all this seeming hopelessness, she still did not give in to outright despair.

Chapter 7

PAINFUL SEPARATION

The main party of captors and captured, still moving on, soon came to Upper Sandusky. At this oasis in the wilderness there was a flourishing mission of between two and three hundred Wyandot church members and a school for the instruction of Indian children in English literature. How advanced these islands of civilization and humanity seemed to those who had experienced nothing but deprivation for weeks on end! Here they met up with an acquaintance from Washington County, Moses Macklewain, who had been taken prisoner from Redstone earlier but had escaped and was on his way home. This generous man not only prayed for release of the white prisoners, but also jeopardized his own life by stealing two strings of corn from the Indians and giving them to the captives. A string of corn was the term applied to thirty or forty ears tied together by a piece of husk and thrown over a pole to dry in its milky state. It was considered a delicacy when boiled, being compared favorably with fresh roasting ears.

The prisoners remained at Sandusky for a few days; but the refreshment of physical rest and food hardly compensated for the loss of loved ones. One of the reasons for their stay was to satisfy the curiosity of the local squaws and their children, none of whom had ever beheld so many white prisoners. Realization of this fact detracted from any credit the captives might mentally have given their captors for the respite they enjoyed from the rigors of the trail. Soon they were off again, this time heading for what were known as the Delaware sugar camps.

These sugar camps were situated on Mill Creek, a branch of the Scioto River, in what became known later as Logan County in Ohio. The main party reached the camps after two more days of painful travel. Meanwhile, shortly after leaving Sandusky, another group of Indians separated from the main company and took with them Mrs. Harden and her remaining child, Mrs. Dowler, and a servant—a black girl who had worked for Mrs. Reynolds for several years. Gradually the body of prisoners was thus being fractionated into more and more helpless units.

The season of making sugar was almost over, but many Indian families were still at this location, along with a number of their warriors. Upon approaching the place, the war party accompanying the prisoners raised a war whoop. Those in the camp responded to the cry which was apparently a signal for another gauntlet, the third thus far suffered by the captives. This time Mrs. Malott was severely beaten with a bridle and sustained a serious open wound from the bits which struck her sharply on the head. The children took more blows than usual on this occasion, mostly at the hands of the Indians' boys and girls, who indulged their misguided passions with the example of the savagery of their parents. Fortunately for Elizabeth Reynolds and her valiant sister, Mary, one of the Indians who had been present at the original capture took their hands, led them to the Indian council house without their being struck, and turned them over to their mother. Conditions had been such that a move like this was most appreciated. Margaret found herself in the position of being grateful for any exemption from any hardship.

Again there was a less painful respite from the rigors of recent weeks. They were permitted to remain at this site for two weeks, residing in the council house, a kind of ceremonial town center for an Indian tribe. It was a crude structure by colonial standards, consisting of loosely fitted logs and skins for protection against the elements and, to be sure, a dirt floor—but one that had been swept comparatively clean. Again, the stay seemed to be in large measure a gratification of the desire of the local populace to exult over a contingent of white prisoners. The Indians celebrated by engaging in wild dances every night, the men first, then the squaws. In the daytime the Indian women would take Mrs. Reynolds and Mrs. Malott and go in quest of hoppenys (a small wild potato), which became their main subsistence during the sojourn at this spot.

Margaret was still in possession of five of her children, three girls and two boys. Joseph and John had already been taken from her, and their whereabouts was still a mystery. Of all her children, though, she felt that it was most important to keep her daughters, trusting that at least the older boys might be better able to take care of themselves and be far less susceptible to gross violation at the mercy of unscrupulous savages. But, as one might surmise, Margaret's wishes were of no more interest to the Indians than the resistance of a cow would be. Indeed, she and her children had been treated—with rare exceptions—with as little respect for their wishes and feelings as if they had been a herd of dumb animals.

Margaret had an intimation from one of the squaws that she might lose some more of her children. So it was not a total surprise, though nonetheless heartrending, when at the end of the two weeks the main party started for Fort Detroit, leaving behind not only the old Delaware chief but also Elizabeth, age eight, and little William, scarcely three and a half,

A less painful respite from rigors of the forced march

along with the one remaining servant girl known as
Scotch Sally. Again, Margaret had not the privilege
of a farewell embrace. The three were hauled off
abruptly by one of the squaws, with the same lack of
feeling as had characterized the other separations.
The children were taken to the Delaware towns
which were situated where the present town of
Delaware is located on the Scioto River.

And now, with such information as is available,
what was life like for little William and Elizabeth in
their enforced captivity? The Scioto River bottom,
an extensive and exceedingly fertile area, was a prime
corn-raising location. The chief of the town where
the children were taken was called Peter by the prisoners, the same chief who had been head of the
initial raiding party and had accompanied the group
until now. But we have no record of what kind of
person he was. William and Scotch Sally were retained
by the chief as his property, but he gave Elizabeth
to his wife's sister, who was married to a man of
rather benign disposition and who had no children
of her own. These characteristics of her would-be
"foster parents" were obviously fortunate for Elizabeth's welfare.

Elizabeth's new home, a wigwam of measurable
superiority over any other in the community except
that of the chief, was not far from the chief's dwelling,
where she occasionally had the pleasure of seeing her

little brother. Besides Sally, the chief also had enslaved a Mrs. Cowen, who had been captured in Kentucky. It was the duty of these two females to raise the corn and attend to all the drudgery of every kind. Here in the same town they also found Peter Malott, one of Mrs. Malott's sons.

When the season for planting corn arrived, all the women, red and white, were expected to break the sod with hoes. No plows were in use, and the males usually lounged in the shade of a tree or bathed in the water at their ease while the women toiled in the hot sun. One old squaw at this Delaware town, not having sufficient help of her own to plant her corn, organized a "party" or semi-social affair to which her neighbors were invited. Each squaw, bringing her own hoe, bowl, and spoon, would deposit the latter two items in the old woman's wigwam and then proceed to the fields to hoe the soil and plant the corn. From this chore the proprietess was able to abstain, but she had been busy preparing a bounteous feast of blue corn boiled very soft, with both broth and kernels retained in the same pot. When the visitors returned from the fields they had their bowls filled with this gruel and, in utter silence, fed themselves to satisfaction. This one-dish meal was all that was "needful," to use a term common among the early writers on this period, and it was usually much better than most of the Indian women were able otherwise to enjoy. In the early summer season when Elizabeth arrived on the scene, she was a guest at this repast and was treated by the old squaw and the other women with the same respect shown to each other.

Shortly after this period, namely mid-summer of 1779, another near-famine plagued the village. Their corn harvest was not yet in, the previous year's stock had been depleted, and the entire community was obliged to subsist on boiled herbage. Elizabeth's master, or her "foster father" if we take into account his relatively kindly nature, at one point took Elizabeth with him on a brief hunting expedition and returned with one turkey. Since this meat did not last long, he secured the help of a nephew, and along with him, his wife, and Elizabeth set out to find a better hunting ground. A two to three day trek over open country was necessary to reach such a place. Encamping on the banks of a small but deep stream, which seems to fit the conditions of the Little Miami, they had almost immediate good luck. The very first day of hunting produced two deer.

Again great joy pervaded the tiny group, including the half-starved little captive. After digging an oblong pit in the ground and filling it with green wood, Elizabeth's master allowed an ensuing fire to reduce the wood to a bed of hot coals. While his nephew tended this and eventually laid sticks across the pit, forming a kind of grill, the master was carefully carving up the venison into thin slices so that, when laid across the grill, they would dry out in a few hours. This process was known as "jirking," and the meat thus dried was called "jirk."*

Needless to say, the first day's hunting experience was repeated, so that in about two weeks they had amassed as much dried venison as their horses could carry. During this period Elizabeth was treated very kindly by her childless "foster mother." In fact, some degree of maternal affection was beginning to show. Among other evidences of this was the squaw's concern for a serious wound on Elizabeth's scalp, which had festered following the effects of the last gauntlet. It had become more and more sore and, according to Elizabeth's own recollection, was even infected with tiny worms. To counter this condition, the squaw first applied some herbs and then carefully rubbed the child's head with bear's oil and combed her hair with a fine-tooth comb. Then she immersed her head in the cold stream and continued to rub it thoroughly. By repeating this process daily she cured her in less than two weeks. The therapy had been applied none too soon, for continuation of the infection much longer would surely have taken the plucky little girl's life.

---

*Today, "jerky."

Some degree of maternal affection

PAINFUL SEPARATION

At last they returned to the Delaware town after their successful hunt and Elizabeth was able to see her little brother again. Had such expressions been in use at the time, one might have said that while Elizabeth's personal condition was "looking up," that of young William was still "in the doldrums." For the little fellow had not forgotten that he was a captive and separated from his mother and friends. He had not become reconciled to his captors or their mode of life and clearly expressed his discontent through frequent crying and fits of screaming. Instead of resorting to any kind of corporal punishment, the chief's wife would simply strip off his clothes and douse him, head to heel, in the cold river. It is hardly necessary to conclude that the result was, in the short run, one of considerable quiet in his demeanor and, in the long run, a perhaps unintended boon to his good health.

Chapter 8

JOYFUL REUNION

About mid-fall another great Indian war party returned to the Delaware village area and the portion of it that passed through the town brought with them a white woman they had captured in Kentucky. This woman had an opportunity, at one point, not only of observing Elizabeth but also of speaking with her alone. The good lady inquired as to her name, place of origin, her relatives, and the circumstances that led to her presence with these Indians. To all of this Elizabeth gave the fullest answers she could and, considering her tender eight years of age, added the following touching plea: "If ever you should get away from the Indians, do send word to my uncles, Joseph Reynolds and Robert Smith, of Washington County, and let them know that brother William and I are here; for I know they will take us back from the Indians. And if you should ever hear of Father [she evidently believed it possible for him to have recovered from the shooting and had not been really aware of the scalping coup de grace], oh tell him where we are!"

A new kind of employment now demanded the attention of Elizabeth. A succession of rains while the hunting party was gone had produced more ears of corn than had been anticipated, but the birds and dogs had begun to inflict serious damage on them. To counter this, the Indians constructed a scaffold about twenty feet in height and consisting of four long poles deeply planted in the ground and lashed together for firmness, topped with a small platform. It was Elizabeth's assignment to ascend this structure every morning (she climbed by means of notches in one of the poles) and, staying there from early morning until dark, to howl and make all the noise in her power to scare the birds and vermin away from the corn field. Once the birds had gone to roost, she was permitted to go home to the village.

After several days of this thankless chore, Elizabeth, unseen by her master or mistress, left her observatory one afternoon in order to gather some crab apples that grew in great abundance on the banks of the river near the corn field. As might be expected, she ate too many, and the acrid qualities of the fruit gave her great pain in the stomach and intestines. It is natural for a child to call for its mother when in distress—and that is exactly what she did. In spite of her full appreciation that her mother was unlikely to

To howl and make all the noise in her power

be near, Elizabeth's emotional state was such that she gave full vent to the possibility that she nevertheless might be and could come to her relief. She could not know that a wilderness of two hundred miles separated them.

Curiously, this painful experience must have been some kind of premonition. For in just a couple of days her mistress, in an obviously fine humor, came to her and, while combing and dressing her hair, made known to her by signs and smiles that two white men had been in town that day and related that her mother was at Fort Detroit, with most of her brothers and sisters. She further managed to get across that she and her husband, Leatherlip and his wife, and Peter Malott, as well as Elizabeth herself, would be going to the Fort as soon as the corn was gathered and that she should then see her mother again. It was the first real ray of hope that had shone upon her cheerless captivity. For days she feasted her imagination upon this prospect of gaining her liberty and being reunited with her mother.

Who these visiting men were she had no idea, but she readily concluded, and accurately, that they had made some agreement with the Indians to take her to her mother. What had happened was that Mrs. Reynolds had prevailed upon Major Dupositer, the commandant of the British forces at Fort Detroit, to send out men with rum to the several Indian towns to try to gather up her children. It was clear that Margaret's practical mind, along with an appreciation of what kind of bait to use, had conceived of at least one way to regain her progeny. And it was indeed two of the Major's men who had visited the town to carry out just such a mission.

Late in the afternoon that very day, Elizabeth's master—himself evidently a temperate man—came out to her perch in the corn field and made clear to her that most of the village's inhabitants were drunk, including his own wife, and that she had better stay out in the field until the orgy was over, lest her own safety be imperiled. Elizabeth readily obeyed and did not leave the field for two nights and a day, surviving on corn which she was able to roast in a fire that her master built for her near her tower. Once the "fire water" intoxicating the Indians was exhausted and order was restored, she was permitted to return to her wigwam at night as usual.

As soon as the corn was ripe and harvested, the little crew named by Elizabeth's mistress set out for Fort Detroit with two horses and a supply of provisions. It was now early October. Sometimes Elizabeth was permitted to ride behind her master, but she had to walk most of the way. One day during the journey a violent storm overtook them. The rain poured in such torrents that their campfires were put out, and the small blanket provided for the child was so inadequate that when she attempted to arise in the morning she found her legs stiff and swollen. From this point on she was stretched out on a horse and thus carried to the river Riche,* four miles south of their destination.

Here the travelers remained for two nights and a day, allowing Elizabeth to recuperate from the worst of her physical misery, and then proceeded into the town for the purpose of trading with a Mr. Baubee, an Indian interpreter and keeper of a public store. The Indians left their little prisoner with this gentleman until they were ready to take her to the council house at the Fort for her redemption. It so happened that Mr. Baubee had a daughter of about Elizabeth's age who had not had any likable playmates for a long time and immediately became attached to her friendly visitor. She even prevailed upon her mother to give Elizabeth an outfit of her clothing, the need for which was obvious to any who had observed the ragged state of the poor child's apparel.

To quote an early chronicler of this occasion, the man who first set down these events from the descriptions of Elizabeth when she was 64 years old: "How important it is that parents should pay particular attention to those early dawnings of philanthropy

---

*This was undoubtedly the River Rouge, the name Riche having been the product of a minor aberration of memory or recording.

in their children, and give it that kind of encouragement that will make it form a distinguishing trait in their character in after life. If there is any virtue that assimilates a human being more to the likeness of God than another, surely it must be genuine philanthropy." And one must add that it did give young Catherine Baubee great satisfaction to see that she had contributed to the comfort and welfare of her new friend. To quote further: "A virtuous action always gives pleasure to its author."

Meanwhile, Margaret Reynolds' situation at Fort Detroit had been the most important turning point in her experience since the fateful ambush on the Ohio. Securing some kind of ransom, the facts of which are not clear, the Indians had left her in the good hands of Major Dupositer, the British officer previously referred to. Officers at the Fort took pity on her plight, having heard her story; and one, a Mr. Buoye, a French gentleman, provided some living space for her in a structure adjacent to his own home, three miles up the river from the Fort. At first Margaret had been quartered at the Fort itself, but upon becoming acquainted with Mrs. Buoye, she received the invitation to reside in more comfortable quarters. Relieved of the immediate physical stress of primitive travel and subsistence, Margaret availed herself of the new time and energy to plan ways to retrieve her children.

When she arrived at the Fort she had only three of her seven children with her—the oldest girl, Mary, who was eleven; the second girl, Sarah, age nine; and Thomas, four and a half. Her first effort was concentrated on Elizabeth, because she was especially mindful, as we have noted, of the need to protect her girls from harm. Therefore, when she approached Major Dupositer to help in reassembling her family, she said, "Sir, I would give anything to get back all of my children at once, but if you must start somewhere first, then I would ask that you try to bargain first of all with the Delaware village in Ohio to return my Elizabeth."

It had been nearly four months since Margaret's youngest daughter had been taken from her, but part of that time had been consumed in her own trek to Fort Detroit. Hence, considering the time necessary to secure her own situation in the Fort area, to permit her negotiations with the military men to give her assistance, and to allow the latter an opportunity to outfit and dispatch scouting expeditions, the return of Elizabeth was really consummated in swift fashion. It appears that what the Major's men had offered her captors was a then usual ransom of one hundred dollars in order to secure her release. Any kind of military intervention or other show of force would have jeopardized the life of the hostage. Hence, the military officers had to exhibit discreet investigation and consummate tact in carrying out their mission. Undoubtedly they had negotiated for release of both Elizabeth and William, but the wily Indians must have decided to test their adversaries by releasing the one child first before they committed themselves to two.

In any event, it was an ecstatic, though tearful, reunion when mother and daughter first saw each other in the council house at the Fort. Margaret was grateful to find that, except for a lameness induced by her recent exposure to the cold rain, Elizabeth appeared to be in relatively good health. Elizabeth made clear to her mother that her period with the Indian family was, for the most part, not too uncomfortable physically speaking and that her master and mistress had on the whole tried to treat her as well as they knew how. For this generosity in the treatment of her child—though in the midst of overall brutality—Margaret did her best to make known to the Indian couple her sincere appreciation. The attachment the squaw had to Elizabeth was again shown when, on their departure, she covered her face with her hands. It was altogether a touching scene. Major Dupositer, who witnessed the event, was himself impressed with the tenderness of the exchange. It steeled him further in his resolve to continue his assistance to the Reynolds family.

Meanwhile, poor little William was still in the Delaware village without even the security of occasionally seeing his beloved big sister. He did not comprehend why she no longer came to him at the chief's wigwam. His mother, as the season was moving into winter, had distressing visions of the little fellow shivering with cold, pallid with want, sitting half-naked in a filthy corner of a smoky wigwam, and in all probability doomed to fall victim to the excesses of a drunken orgy. Such gloomy reflections disturbed every hour of rest or repose she might otherwise have enjoyed. It was now well into December, and the days were getting increasingly cold.

Mrs. Reynolds' anxieties were relieved only in part when, to her astonishment, a Mr. Robinson of Upper Sandusky showed up one day with her son John, next in age to Elizabeth, and the second child who had been snatched from her. Robinson had encountered the child in an Ohio village and, out of pure humanitarian motives, redeemed him and brought him to the Fort. Whether he had to pay the usual rate of tribute was never known, for he refused to put the young mother in his debt. Again, there was a joyful reunion, this one especially emotional because it was so impromptu and unanticipated.

Also, Margaret had on several occasions actually seen her eldest, Joseph, although always too briefly. She had learned some time during the fall that he was with an Indian family in Canada, not too far on the other side of the river near Fort Detroit. Tentative contacts had been made, but no release seemed to be in prospect, for reasons that shall be clear later, but at least the Indians relented enough to bring him to visit his mother. Thus, with the return of Elizabeth and John, the location of all the children was known, and attention could be concentrated on their ultimate release. Nevertheless, the relief afforded by this fact could only partially compensate for the mother's persistent anxiety over the youngest of all—William. But the Major's men had not been idle.

At the same time, Mrs. Reynolds was also occupied with more mundane labors. On her awful journeys before arriving at the Fort she had been deprived of all her best clothing. An old blanket to wear had been given her by her captors, but it would scarcely hold together. When it was torn by brush or limb she would fasten it together as best she could with a thorn or wooden pin. On the afternoon of her first day at the Fort some of the wives of officers, seeing her plight, first offered to give employment to her daughter Mary, then almost twelve. But the proud mother, her spirit still unbroken, could not accept this. Though puzzled by this reaction, the good ladies on the next day sent Margaret a gift of a large bolt of cloth, material of obvious good quality. It was of somber color, perhaps intended for mourning dresses, but Margaret seized upon it as a chance to clothe her family and to make some garments for sale too. She was a good hand with needle and thread, which she borrowed from her benefactors, and was occupied during much of the fall in making shirts, which she sold for two dollars each, as well as in fully reoutfitting her children. Further, as a technical prisoner of war of the British, she drew eight rations a day from the Fort. It was thus that the family was able to make out in a material sense during the months in the Fort area.

On a cold mid-December day, when Elizabeth Reynolds was passing by the council house door on her way to getting a bucket of water, an officer called to her, "Little girl, come here, and you may see your little brother." Throwing her vessel down, she ran inside and there, to her incredible delight, sat little William, his head down, looking altogether like a little Delaware papoose. "Don't speak to him," suggested the officer, "Let's see if he will recognize you."

As Elizabeth approached him the officer said to William, "Do you know this little girl?"

Raising his head and looking intently for a moment, William exclaimed, "It's my Betsy!"

Forgetting her lameness in her excitement, Elizabeth ran like a young deer to the place at the Fort where her mother happened to be at the moment and shouted, "Oh, Mother, William is come! William is come!"

"It's my Mama!"

Startled, but electrified with joy, Margaret, even as she ran, screamed, "Is my poor little son really alive? Is he really here?"

As she and Elizabeth arrived at the council house, again the officer suggested, "See if he knows you." It had been nearly six months since he had seen his mother. When the officer asked him, "Do you know this woman?", William stared even more fixedly than he had at Elizabeth, making a supreme effort to bring this change from his most recent routine into focus.

Then his features changed into a tearful smile, "It's my Mama! It's my Mama!" No oration, no great literary achievement, could have reproduced the eloquence of that response.

The officers immediately paid his redemption, and again our valiant and determined mother was able to enjoy a spirited and joyous reunion. One's youngest is always a little special, and recognition of this fact of family life was given full vent on this occasion. There was boundless rejoicing in the modest Reynolds household that evening. William was too excited to go to sleep at his usual hour. He kept repeating: "My Mama! My Betsy! My Mama! My Betsy!", as if repeating it would somehow reassure him that it was all for real. It took days for a thorough bath, a shampoo and trimming of his hair, and replacement of his crude Indian clothing to give him the appearance of a young frontiersman again. But soon he looked like the little Reynolds chap that he was, albeit an inch or so taller and a few pounds lighter.

Chapter 9

ESCAPE

Finally the family had reached a point where the one remaining problem was securing the release of Joseph from the Canadian tribe. Unlike the other cases of appropriation of the children, this one presented some special difficulties. Joseph was the prisoner of a very old Wyandot chief who had taken such a fancy to the lad that he declared him adopted as his own son and designated the boy to succeed himself as chief. Already he came to be looked upon in the camp as no ordinary personage. He was given status, privileges, and benefits utterly unknown to other prisoners. But, more unpleasantly, he was required to take on some other physical attributes of a future chief. His hair was almost completely shorn and the remainder ornamented with silver brooches. The Indians had even bored a place in his nostrils and inserted a silver jewel. He had pleaded so stoutly for his ears that, so far, they were permitted to go uncut. His special dress consisted of a long robe of fine blue cloth, richly set with jewels of various sizes and colors. It was quite plain that his master had no intention of parting with him.

Fortunately for her peace of mind the cut in Joseph's nose had not yet been made when his mother had seen him in the fall, but she was fully cognizant that his release by ransom was impossible. Furthermore, she learned that Joseph's master and family had gone on a long journey, taking Joseph with them, and they lost complete contact for nine months. By now it was late summer in 1780, and Margaret and her six other children continued to live at the Buoye's, surviving by the rations and by frequent sewing jobs for the families at the Fort. As best she could, Margaret tutored her children in reading, writing, and arithmetic, supplemented by occasional assistance from other adults in the Detroit area. Yet, her principal preoccupation was in devising potential methods by which Joseph could be freed. It was clear that his return would have to be by stratagem.

As soon as Mrs. Reynolds learned of Joseph's return to his camp across the river she began exploring every possible scheme that offered hope of regaining him. Among other news she found that all the male Indians were, for the time being, absent from the camp, and Joseph was left in charge of the squaws. This appeared to offer a rare opportunity. Further, she was aware that on an island in the middle of the river a Captain Riddle, who himself with his family had at one time been Indian captives, had a small establishment in which his family and some acquaintances resided. It occurred to Margaret that this gentleman would very likely be understanding of her concerns.

Thus, she engaged a small row boat to ferry her to Captain Riddle's place and see what final devices she could employ to free Joseph. There she met two white men who agreed to help her in her plot. The next step was for her to go over to Joseph's camp under the pretext of visiting with him. The Indians had never denied her an opportunity for such a visit, and the fact that Joseph had just recently returned from his long absence made it seem all the more reasonable that the two should be allowed a discreet reunion. On the last leg of the trip from the island Margaret rowed alone. The squaws received her without any apparent suspicion of her real design.

After she had been in the camp for perhaps a half hour, Margaret requested Joseph to go to the river and bring her a drink of water. The squaws did not question this. Shortly, Margaret began expressing some uneasiness that he might fall into the river at some precipitous spot and be drowned. The squaws, understanding what she meant, scoffed at her concern and insisted that Joseph was a good swimmer. She nonetheless persisted in her apprehensions and finally went after him. He was returning with the water when she met him. Walking slowly to the camp center, they had ample opportunity to converse without being overheard. This was the point when she was able to communicate her plan to him.

Briefly the plan was this: In a skirt of heavy woods a few hundred yards from the village the two men she had employed were to secret themselves that evening. As soon as it was dark Joseph was to go over to the woods as unpretentiously as possible and listen for a subdued voice calling out his name. He was to run as fast as he could toward the voice, be picked up by the two men, and be rowed as rapidly as possible to the island where Captain Riddle's place was located. From this point on, his mother would take over further maneuvers.

Although the hushed dialogue between mother and son had not aroused any suspicions among the squaws, the prospect of being speedily delivered from his bondage and reunited with his family was so exciting to Joseph that he indulged in a boyish caper that could well have defeated the whole enterprise. On returning to the camp he began skipping about and, ascending a little post near where the women were sitting, exclaimed: "Tonight, and then!" His mother frowned and ordered him down at once. Fortunately, the squaws did not appear to comprehend the meaning of his behavior or his words, so Mrs. Reynolds was finally able to depart with the hope that her rescue plan was still intact.

When night came on, Joseph managed to get over to the woods without creating any concern on the part of the squaws and waited until it was thoroughly dark. For a while he heard nothing and, discouraged, had just turned to get back to the village before he was missed when he finally heard a soft but distinct call: "Joseph!" He raced to the source of the sound, found the two men, and was quickly conveyed to the Riddle island where his mother boarded. They then proceeded not only across the river to the American side but up the stream for an additional nine miles to a Mrs. Cassady's place. Margaret had made previous arrangements with this lady who already had experience in aiding the escape of prisoners and had several very secure hiding spots in her establishment. There she left Joseph temporarily while she returned back downstream for six miles to the Buoye residence and her other children. The good men from the Riddle place, having completed their job, were dismissed by Mrs. Reynolds with a gift of new shirts, which was all she could scrounge up as a reward.

It was not surprising that the very next morning, perceiving their loss and fearful of the wrath of the chief and his men when they returned, a committee of squaws showed up at Mrs. Buoye's house and complained bitterly against Mrs. Reynolds, accusing her of having "stolen" her own son. In their psychology he was their rightful spoils of war, giving no thought to the fact that their menfolk had made an unprovoked attack and commandeered a helpless crew of travelers. To them, banditry was what war was all about. It was not a contest over territory; it was simply taking any opportunity to waylay strangers and relieve them of any goods or persons they took a fancy to.

Mrs. Reynolds was not present when this visitation took place, but the squaws made very clear that unless Joseph were returned very soon they would inflict all kinds of harm on her and her children. Little Elizabeth, observing the confrontation, could not refrain from a triumphal cry: "Hah, mother has got Joe!" Mrs. Buoye shushed her, but the angry squaws would not be stopped from searching high and low for the boy. They combed every nook and cranny in the house and on the premises and, frustrated by their failure, began grabbing the other children to take as hostages. But the heroic youngsters fought and screamed so fiercely that the would-be kidnappers could not hang on to them. They finally left empty-handed, shouting imprecations and threats in their own language that by their mere sound seemed ominously fearful.

When Mrs. Reynolds returned just a few minutes after they were out of sight, she immediately decided that the Buoye residence was no longer a safe place for her children. She and the six thereupon took off at once for the Fort, three miles distant. To forestall discovery she separated the youngsters into two groups, placing three in the care of a friend and the other three inside the Fort at a Mr. Williams' house.

The men of the Indian village had apparently not been too far away from their homes, for the squaws must have gotten word to them about the escape, with the result that early on the very next morning Joseph's former master and a contingent of his men arrived at Fort Detroit and demanded of Major Dupositer that he surrender the boy, at the same time continuing to threaten Mrs. Reynolds and her other children. The Major told them that he knew nothing about the whereabouts of the lad and, with tongue in cheek, stated that if the accusation were true he must punish Mrs. Reynolds for her temerity.

Hardly satisfied by this response, the Indians then proceeded to ransack the Fort and the surrounding town, eventually reaching Mr. Williams' home, where Elizabeth, William, and John were being cared for. Luckily the children had seen their would-be captors coming and had time to crawl under the porch floor, a tactic they undertook of their own accord. Their consciousness of danger was sufficient incentive for them to keep breathlessly quiet—to quote a favorite of the times, "as quiet as mice when the cat is about the barn." While the Indians were asking about Mrs. Reynolds and searching the house, a girl who lived with the Williams' secreted the three children from their temporary concealment, took them to a nearby warehouse, locked them in it, put the key in her pocket, and dropped out of sight.

Frustrated again, the Indians returned to Major Dupositer and renewed their complaints. But this time, with little delay, they decided to take matters more pointedly into their own hands. They canoed up the river from the Fort, stopping at every house on both sides to continue their frantic search. At the Cassady's the trusty proprietess had so thoroughly concealed Joseph that the search was fruitless. As soon as the Indians were again out of sight, our sagacious mother Reynolds transferred the three children in her friend's care to the Williams warehouse and therefore had all six safely lodged within its confines.

Then Major Dupositer sent for her to inquire what knowledge she had about her son's escape. She went to this interrogation with only the mildest apprehension, for she did not wish to be impertinent to the officer who had been so generous in providing the resources and diplomatic means to rescue two of her children. But, she was nonetheless resolved not to give in to any intimidation that a military man might feel was necessary to conform with some stuffy and inhuman "rule" of war. Hence she confessed at his first question that she had contrived Joseph's escape herself and took full responsibility.

"That was a mighty daring act for a woman," observed the commanding officer.

"Perhaps," she replied, "but what will not a mother do to free her child from Indian captivity?"

"Very true; I fully understand," he responded. "But in my position I must threaten you before the Indians, and if you should hear of it, do not be concerned. There may be some who will try to shake your resolve and spoil your plans, but rest assured I will aid you all I can. But, now, what do you intend doing next?"

"I have all my children, and although I lost my dear husband, I want to get the rest of us to western Maryland as soon as I can."

"Well," the good officer noted, "a ship is sailing from here for Montreal in just a few days. I can fix it so that you and your family can get passage, and I will put necessary provisions on board for all of you."

It was a relief to learn of the prospect of almost immediate departure. The next day Margaret was able to slip her Joseph from the Cassady household to the Williams warehouse and begin preparations for the next great step. It was now deep into fall, over eighteen months from the time her family with the others had set out from Redstone on their ill-starred voyage. "Pray that this next voyage may be more successful!" Margaret thought to herself as she carefully prepared for the final details of getting her crew on board. Just two days later, under cover of night, the entire family along with their meager belongings and the provisions bestowed by the Major, plus ten other persons in the Detroit area, boarded the vessel; they set sail at dawn.

Mrs. Reynolds was, to be sure, greatly indebted to the kind and considerate British Fort commander for all that he had done. There is no telling what might have happened to the family had he not been so cooperative. Very likely at least three of the children would have been lost, and even the prospect of transportation to any place readily accessible to Maryland would have been bleak for all the rest. Her feeling of gratitude to the Major, however, should not be taken to mean that she wavered in her support for the colonial cause in the revolution. Her position on this was well illustrated by an incident that occurred that spring at the Fort. A British Captain named Reynolds was interested in exploring with Margaret whether he could by any chance have been related to her late husband. He said he himself had been born in Maryland. "And what brought you here?" Margaret inquired.

"When the war broke out, I left the colonies and entered the service of the King," he replied.

"Then I have no further desire to trace the relationship," retorted Margaret. "I don't want my children to be associated with a Tory." And so ended the conversation.

One cannot help but wonder whether the good Major had heard of this exchange, for if he did, he deserved all the more credit for his magnanimity. Chances are that the young Captain did not admit to his rebuff. In any event, the faithfulness of our heroine to the revolutionary cause, in spite of her distaste for war and its aftermaths, was unequivocal. It is of interest that when Elizabeth in later life told of the entire adventure—if that be what it can properly be called—she was quick to stress this firm attitude of her mother's about the justice of the American cause and her repugnance not against the British but against those colonists who failed to support the new United States of America.

Returning to the thread of our narrative, it might well be supposed that the determined Indians had not yet given up. When they observed at a distance the departure of the ship, they were crafty enough to suspect that their quarry was aboard and so set out in their war canoes to pursue it. And they did not give up until the vessel had escaped them at Niagara.

Being in canoes they had to follow the coast of the lakes instead of taking the shortest route, so they could not always keep the ship in sight. Even so, the ship was only twelve hours ahead of them at Niagara—which nevertheless was a safe enough margin to insure it against attack. And so, our little party of refugees made good their escape.

Determined Indians had not yet given up

Chapter 10

AND SO TO HOME

One might conclude that, having escaped the clutches of Indian aggrandizement, the Reynolds family experienced no further problems. From a comparative standpoint this was true. Certainly any obstacles or diversions that complicated the final return of the family to a more untroubled agrarian existence could not compare in severity with those that plagued its previous year and a half of violence and deprivation. Nevertheless the remainder of its trip back to western Maryland—which is obviously where all the Reynolds wanted to go—was by no means uneventful.

Aside from matters of payment for passage, to which they were indebted mainly to the good British Major Dupositer, they had other hurdles to surmount. Upon arrival in Montreal, as per instruction from her Fort Detroit benefactors, Mrs. Reynolds called on the Commanding General of the British forces at that station. It turned out that he and most of his officers were German. Although Mrs. Reynolds could understand German (an interesting talent for a frontierswoman of English descent), she did not feel herself competent to speak it. Fortunately there was among the entourage in her ship a Dutch lady who was fluent in German. Taking her along as an interpreter, Margaret Reynolds was able to negotiate from the General permission to travel to the new United States via the rest of the St. Lawrence waterway and around the Atlantic to the New England states.

But this privilege necessitated a wait of some days for a permit and passport to arrive from Quebec City. During this stay Margaret learned of several American officers who were incarcerated in the local British prison as detainees of war. One of them, a Captain Stokely, had been an acquaintance of hers from Maryland. Hence she took it upon herself to visit him in prison while she was awaiting her travel documents. At this contact she learned that Stokely and two of his companions were in an especially difficult position because they had unsuccessfully attempted an escape.

"If we had not got lost in the wilderness," explained the Captain, "we would have made good our freedom. Our main lack was a compass." Taking note of this, Margaret began contriving how she might smuggle a compass to Stokely to aid him in a further escape trial. She scoured the shops near the waterfront in Montreal until she finally spied some compasses. Not wishing to arouse suspicions about her motives, she first bought a few inconsequential articles in the shop and then remarked to her companion, pointing to the compasses, "Oh, look at those beautiful snuff boxes!" Although the proprietor tried to explain their real purpose, Margaret would have none of this and insisted on flaunting her spurious ignorance by saying that she wanted two of them for toys for her two youngest boys. Totally outmaneuvered, the shopkeeper readily sold the items; and that very afternoon Margaret managed to secret the two compasses in the prison to Captain Stokely. Little did she know that the night her three countrymen planned their renewed escape effort, armed with these new essential instruments for travel, they received news of termination of the revolutionary conflict, thus insuring their early release.

Meanwhile, the papers from Quebec had arrived, so that the Reynolds family along with nineteen other Americans set sail for the United States. At one point they were all searched for letters or papers in their possession, but one escaped their attention. This had been a letter, concealed in the ample hair of the enterprising Margaret Reynolds, written from an American prisoner in Montreal to his wife. And, almost needless to say, our plucky messenger did eventually deliver the hidden missive to its addressee.

After a few days, the ship landed at a place called East Bay in what was then part of Vermont. Here the passengers, all technically still in prisoner-of-war status, were handed over to their own countrymen. From here they were taken by further water conveyance to Saratoga, then Albany, and finally New York. Somewhere on the East River they were able to meet with General Washington, who supplied them with papers that would insure their return to any point where friends or relatives could assume responsibility. The next and final port was Philadelphia. Here Mrs. Reynolds was able to hire a wagon to transport her family on its final leg of the lengthy, tiresome journey. It took eight days, over primitive, rough roads, to reach western Maryland where their relatives still resided.

On midafternoon of that eighth wearisome day, a small boy stepped on the porch of the old home of Captain John Reynolds' parents, Margaret's father- and mother-in-law. "And whose little boy are you?" asked Grandfather Reynolds.

Little William, still less than five, hardly appreciating the profound impact his words would have, answered proudly: "Captain John Reynolds!"

Looking down the road a few yards the astonished grandparents saw Margaret and the other six children slowly walking from where they had left the wagon.

"And whose little boy are you?"

They could scarcely believe their eyes. Except for their son John himself, of whose loss they had already been informed by the military party that had discovered the bodies on the drifting barge nineteen months before, they were able to embrace every member of the valiant family.

For once during the better part of two years Margaret Reynolds was able to relax—without feeling that everyone's welfare was a weighty responsibility of hers alone. Only a homecoming like this could help ease the pain of the family's many months of deprivation and the anguish of their loss of husband and father. Only this relatively happy conclusion to their lengthy trials could remind them of those to whom they owed so much—the friendly Moravian and other Christian Indians; the generous "enemy" officer, the British Major Dupositer; the Buoye family and others at Fort Detroit; the scouts who retrieved Margaret's children; and, most of all, that unseen Hand that maintained their basic health and resourcefulness in spite of all the obstacles that nature and man put before them.

Courage and intelligence—these were qualities so often required on the frontier. And it was these attributes with which the Reynolds family and their friends, but above all Margaret Reynolds, were so richly endowed. All of us are surely the better for it. And so is our nation.

EPILOGUE

After several years of readjustment Margaret remarried in 1785. The man who took over as father in the household was William Baird. He had been a member of the Provincial Congress, representing the Upper District of Frederick, Maryland, then a part of Washington County.

From this union Margaret had two more children. It was one of these, Frances, from whom my wife is descended. Margaret Reynolds Baird was my wife's great-great-great grandmother.

All the Reynolds and Baird children grew to adulthood and prospered, some moving to other parts of the expanding young country. A brother of Captain John, enraged by the unfortunate experiences of his relatives, devoted almost all his life to feats of revenge, becoming one of the celebrated Indian fighters of the area.

It is understood that eventually the Harden and Malott families were also reunited, but each had lost one child. Among all the Americans taken prisoner during this period by the northwestern Indians, the

Reynolds family was the only one known to writers of the day which, after the initial loss of the father, was able to wrest itself intact from captivity. Coupled with providential strokes of good fortune, along with all their setbacks, no small measure of reason for this success was the fortitude, skill, and determination of Margaret Reynolds. One can hardly overestimate the significance of these qualities. For such was the caliber of character and stamina that helped propel a young nation into a state of freedom, prosperity, and leadership unmatched in human history.